# While We S

## Contents

# In the Dark

While you are asleep at night, some people are at work. Night workers do many important jobs. They sleep during the day.

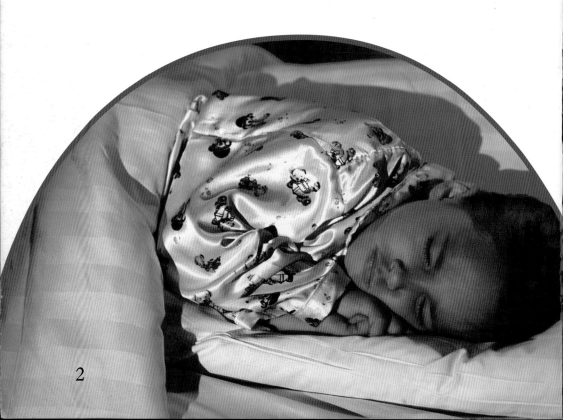

Can you think of some reasons
why people need to work at night?

# Clean Sweep

Many cleaners work at night. They clean streets, offices and shops while it is quiet and there are not many people around.

# Safe Travel

Road workers keep our roads safe to drive on. They often repair roads during the night when there is very little traffic.

Some railway workers work at night, too. They fix train tracks and railway signals so that trains can travel safely.

MEN
WORKING

# Night Moves

People often have to travel at night. They rely on night workers to get them wherever they want to go.

Many cab drivers work all night. People are also needed to drive trains and buses. Pilots fly planes at night, too.

# Door-to-Door

Many goods, such as fresh food and newspapers, have to be delivered every day. Some truck drivers work through the night to make sure that these goods arrive on time.

# Food for the Day

Some people work in supermarkets during the night. They make sure the shelves are full for the next day.

Most bakers start work while it is still dark. They bake at night so that the bread will be fresh when it goes on sale in the morning.

13

# Night News

News stories don't only happen during the day. Some reporters need to work during the night to make sure that all the news is up to date.

Many people who work on morning newspapers have to work at night. There are stories to write and newspapers to print and deliver.

# Health Workers

Hospital patients need to be looked after twenty-four hours a day. Many doctors, nurses and other health workers need to work at night.

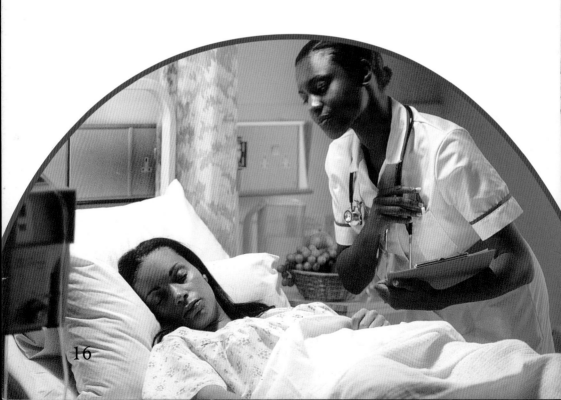

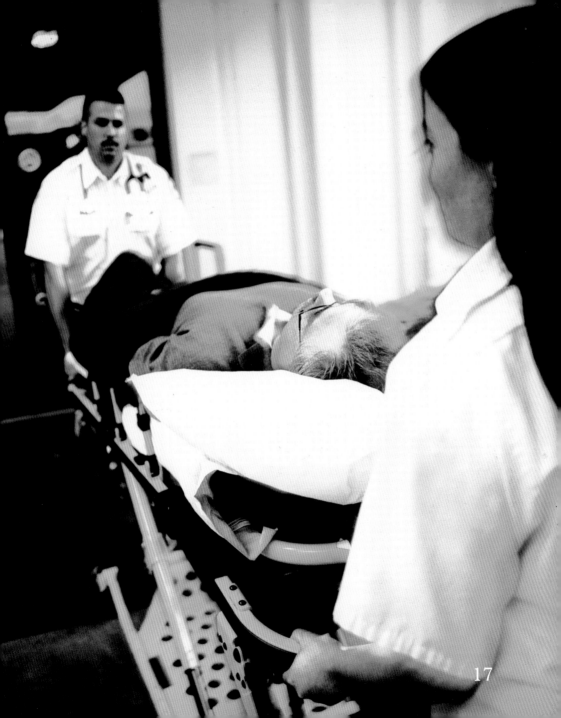

# Emergency!

Fires, accidents and other emergencies can happen at any time. So there are always firefighters, police and ambulance workers on duty.

# Sky Watch

Stars and planets can be seen most clearly at night. Astronomers and other sky watchers use telescopes and computers to track the night sky.

# Night Lights

Firework displays take place at night. The workers set up their equipment during the day—but they must wait until it is dark to put on their spectacular shows.

# Index